Community-Based Participatory Action Research

Community-Based Participatory Action Research

IT'S ALL ABOUT THE COMMUNITY

Bruce D. Friedman

The University of Texas at El Paso

cognella®

SAN DIEGO

Bassim Hamadeh, CEO and Publisher
Amy Smith, Project Editor
Casey Hands, Production Editor
Jess Estrella, Senior Graphic Designer
Stephanie Kohl, Licensing Coordinator
Natalie Piccotti, Director of Marketing
Kassie Graves, Vice President of Editorial
Jamie Giganti, Director of Academic Publishing

Cover image: Copyright © 2018 iStockphoto LP/naqiewei.

Printed in the United States of America.

cognella® | ACADEMIC PUBLISHING
3970 Sorrento Valley Blvd., Ste. 500, San Diego, CA 92121

Contents

PREFACE

I N THE SOCIAL sciences, one of the required courses is research; however, many students truly do not understand the purpose or function of the research process. Research is about inquiry, about finding an answer. Some may call it a critical thinking inquiry, or a way to dig deeper into understanding. Sure, we can look at things from face value and accept them as they are, or we can seek to understand. For me, I prefer to dig deeper to understand, but does the solution only have meaning to me or is there a larger community who cares about the answer?

Basic university research seems to be purely done for the sake of answering a question. There is usually very little interaction between the investigator and the community. But who really cares about the answer? Is there an action to follow the research or does it sit on the shelves of a university in the dissertation section with only the dissertation chair and the committee ever reading the content? Few dissertations have much of a wide reach. That is partially because there is little community engagement, and the only one who cares is the researcher.

That has been outside my personal way of thinking. Of course, I have a natural sense of inquiry, but usually that sense of inquiry is to develop a deeper understanding of what will help people, what will help the community.

But helping the community is not an easy feat. The first step is figuring out how to help the community, or even before that figure out who the community is. There is the adage that those who win the wars write the history books; however, what happens to those communities who are swept up by the dominant community as a result of losing the war? Does anyone ever hear from them? This is an issue that relates to years of discriminatory practices, which will not be addressed in this book, but it raises the issue of how we define community. Chapter 3 of this book will provide some tools for community mapping, for community mapping has become more complicated as a result of technology and communities are no longer defined by geographic location. Therefore, it is more important to be clear about how we define the members of the community with whom we are engaging.

Finding meaning in a community advocating for change involves engaging that community and listening to them to truly understand the issues that are being addressed. Once we can engage the community, then we can develop a research plan with action steps that will lead to a change process.

The extent that the community is engaged in research follows a continuum, as depicted by Figure 0.1. The more the community becomes a partner in the research plan and is integrated into the research plan, the greater and more meaningful the change.

In some respects, it is similar to the way a clinician works with a client since the clinician cannot change the client but works with the client in order that the client assumes responsibility for changing. Through community-engaged research, the researcher partners with the community to bring about meaningful change. Thus, by working with larger systems and communities, it is possible to apply some of those same skills but in a positive way to help a community take action to address the larger problems that are being faced.

This book is a development of my collective experiences of working with communities. What I have learned through this process was the more engaged I was with the community, the mutual change process for all participants was more meaningful. The solutions become community solutions that will continue once I have gone. I have learned that it is not about me, but it is about the community.

Community-Based Participatory Action Research is the highest form of community engagement and community involvement. It is not easy, but the steps presented in Chapter 5 make the process manageable and doable. Regardless of your practice level, engaging community members and developing a comprehensive community-based participatory action research project will help the community make a lasting change and help you find meaning in yourself.

	Basic Research Outside of Community Involvement	Community-Placed Research	Basic Community Partnership Research	Close Community Partnership Research	Community-Based Participatory Research (CBPR)	Community-Based Participatory Action Research (PAR)
Definition	• University researcher-initiated project • No interactive relationship between investigator and community	• (University) researcher-initiated project • One time or short-term relationship between investigator and community • Limited community involvement beyond venue	• Project based on a relationship with a community partner • (University) researcher makes key decisions in consideration of needs and interests of community • Dissemination of outcomes to community	• Ongoing collaborative project • Goals co-defined to balance benefit to (university) researcher and utility of findings for community • Research methodology primarily determined by (university) researcher	• Project defined by co-creation of project ideas and procedures by (university) researchers and community • Substantive participation by community in all stages • Shared governance • Expectation to use findings to change systems or solve community problems	• Project defined by co-inquiry team of university and community participants • Integration of participation, inquiry (research), and action by all participants to bring about meaningful and mutual change for all participants
Examples	• Secondary data analysis of reading program scores	• One-time community survey of children's reading ability	• Tracking children's reading abilities over time in cooperating school	• Long-term collaborative project to improve reading scores in school	• Co-created community intervention to improve community capacity for reading program at library	• Co-created research initiative of parents, students, school, & university researchers to improve reading in school that results in policy and practice change

FIGURE 0.1. Community Engaged Research.

Acknowledgments

This book is an expression of the love for inquiry and the love for community. By helping others seek to understand, I feel a deeper sense of accomplishment.

I would also like to thank the staff at Cognella Academic Publishing for believing in me to publish this book and Kassie Graves, the vice president of acquisitions.

Image Credits

Fig. 0.1: Adapted from Darlyne Bailey, et al., "Community Engaged Research," The Alignment of Leadership Development and Participatory Action Research (PAR): One Process and Product From the University Northside Partnership. Copyright © 2009 by University of Minnesota.

CHAPTER 1

Participatory Research

It Is All About the Community

S TUDENTS IN THE social sciences seem to veer away from research courses even though they are a required part of the curriculum (Friedman, 2017). This raises questions about why there is such an aversion to research courses. Faculty see the value in research, which is the rationale for it being part of a curriculum; however, it seems that there is a disconnect between the value faculty place on research and the value the students have on the content.

From a faculty perspective, research is a logical thinking process for problem solving. There is a problem or question and research demonstrates a methodology for arriving at an answer. Much of that problem-solving process involves using large sets of data with numbers associated with them, and it is the analysis of those number sets that are used to arrive at another number that is used to address the problem. Thus, is the problem with the process, with the use of numbers, or something completely different from either of those?

On the other hand, students who enter the social sciences usually have a certain value set that focuses on either helping people or wanting to enhance some type of change process. Either way, helping or being part of a change does not appear to be equal to a quantitative approach to research methods that uses numbers and statistics to demonstrate whether something is significant to accept or reject a hypothesis or guess of what would be seen in the environment. There does not appear to be a logical fit between course content and personal values for entering a social science discipline. This lack of disconnect between values and course content might be explained by aspects of adult learning styles.

Based on Knowles's (1980) ideas, there are seven basic principles that relate to adult learning. These principles are (a) Adults are self-directed; (b) there is a rationale for why adults need to learn the content; (c) adults should be involved in setting their own learning objectives; (d) adults learn in an environment of mutual trust; (e) adults learn from their own experiences and the experiences of others; (f) the acquired knowledge can be immediately used or applied; and (g) adults should be actively involved in both the learning and evaluation of that learning (Friedman, 2013). Thus, when looking at a research methods or statistics course, the problem is not with the intent of the course, but rather there is a value disconnect between how faculty approach the course and whether students are able to appreciate the value behind the course in addressing their own personal values and needs. Action research is a methodological change that will address the value disconnect. A brief description of action research addresses how this research process brings together the two different value systems of faculty and the students or learners to create a more meaningful learning process.

To begin understanding action research, it is important to first define social sciences. Levin and Greenwood (2011) describe social sciences as "a form of contextualized institutional social practice" (p. 27). They further define social sciences as a way to examine organizational structures, power relations, discourses, and external relations that relate to a change process. They describe four important elements that should be included in the social science research process. These four elements involve, first, a multi-perspective research approach that includes relevant social science, humanistic, and scientific levels of understanding. Second, there is a level of methodological diversity involving quantitative, qualitative, and mixed methods approaches. Third, research should include stakeholders. Fourth, there needs to be an emphasis on the relevance to addressing social problems (Levin & Greenwood, 2011).

The relationship between how students learn as described by Knowles and how Levin and Greenwood define the social sciences and social science research seems to resonate. There appears to be a consistency in learning what is relevant and important in both, and action research is a research methodology to begin to address both, raising the question "Why are the various forms of action research not used more whole-heartedly?" Rather than trying to address the why question, it might be better to identify what action research is.

Although the emphasis of this book is on community-based participatory action research (CBPAR), it is important to understand the basic elements of action research. Action research encompasses a methodological approach that links practice and research in a form of action. The history of the various types of action research will be presented in the next chapter, but this chapter will focus on the philosophy behind actions research, moving to the proposed form of CBPAR, which is an outgrowth of earlier forms of action research.

Action research is a very dynamic form of research, with the key element being that the research encompasses some level of action. In essence, that action comes in three different forms. There is research for action, research in action, and research on action. What these three terms mean is that there are three entry points to engage in the research process. Research for action is research to understand a problem in order to take action. When you think of research in action, this refers to a monitoring process of an ongoing action and taking corrective measures along the way in order to achieve the desired results. Research on action refers to the evaluation of a particular action that has been taken. What these three concepts demonstrate is that action research involves opportunities for reflection along the way and opportunities for adjustments. An action researcher has multiple opportunities and entry points to be able to participate in the research process, and that makes it very dynamic. What it also suggests is that there is constant opportunity for feedback, suggesting that there are others outside of oneself who are accountable for the research process. Thus, action research engages others in the process and is not a stagnant form of research that appears to exist when reading and reviewing many research studies.

Expanding on this concept more fully, action research is a systemic inquiry that involves collective, collaborative, self-reflective, and critical analyses that are undertaken by participants (McCutcheon & Jung, 1990). These analyses are conducted within a social situation in order to improve the social conditions and social justice situation within that environment. Action research contributes to the practical concerns of people to redress a problematic situation with a goal of joint collaboration in a mutually acceptable ethical framework (Rapaport, 1970).

As such, four themes emerge: participant empowerment, collaboration, knowledge acquisition, and social change. The process is a spiral process involving planning, acting, observing, and reflecting as diagramed by Kemmis and McTaggart (2007). As Figure 1.1 identifies, the process is constantly moving forward; however, there is continual planning and reflecting based on the observations of

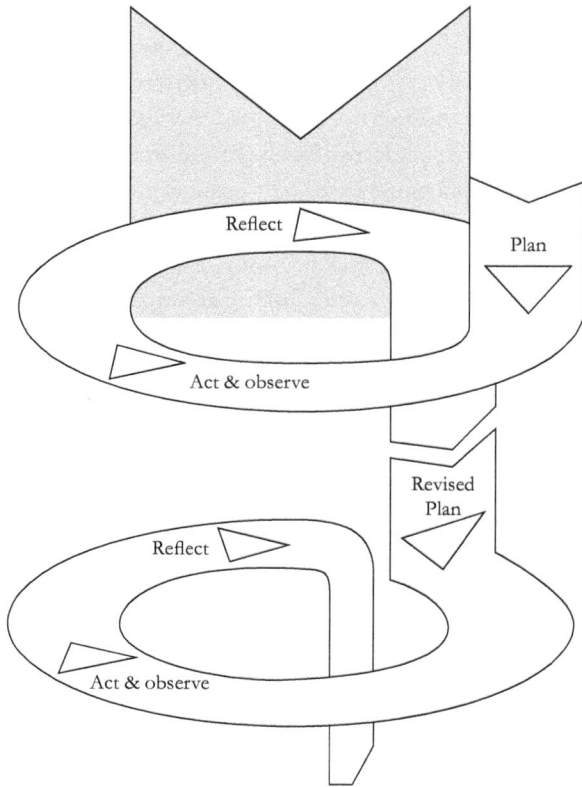

FIGURE 1.1. The Action Research Spiral.

the actions. Thus, rather than a straight line forward, it is a spiral resulting from the constant changing nature of the actions.

In thinking about action research, then, three minimal factors should be in place. There should be a goal for improvement with people who are willing to be involved in a change process. As Grundy and Kemmis (1981) state, the three requirements are as follows:

1. The project takes as its subject matter a social practice, regarding it as a strategic action susceptible to improvement

2. The project proceeds through a spiral of cycles of planning, acting, observing and reflecting, with each of these activities being systematically and self-critically implemented and interrelated

3. The project involves those responsible for the practice in each of the moments of the activity, widening participation in the project gradually

to include others affected by the practice and maintaining collaborative control of the process

Since action research is a reflective process that uses social interactions to transform, a number of social constructs are at work during each phase of the process. These social constructs are in the form of the culture and language of the target system. There will be more about target systems when we discuss community, but for now it is important to consider all unique aspects of that target system when reflecting on the action or change process that is being addressed. These social constructs come in the form of language, culture, how power is defined, various skill sets that are being used, values and norms of that community, and other unique factors that differentiate that particular target system or community from others. Thus, a more accurate depiction of the transformative process could be depicted by Figure 1.2.

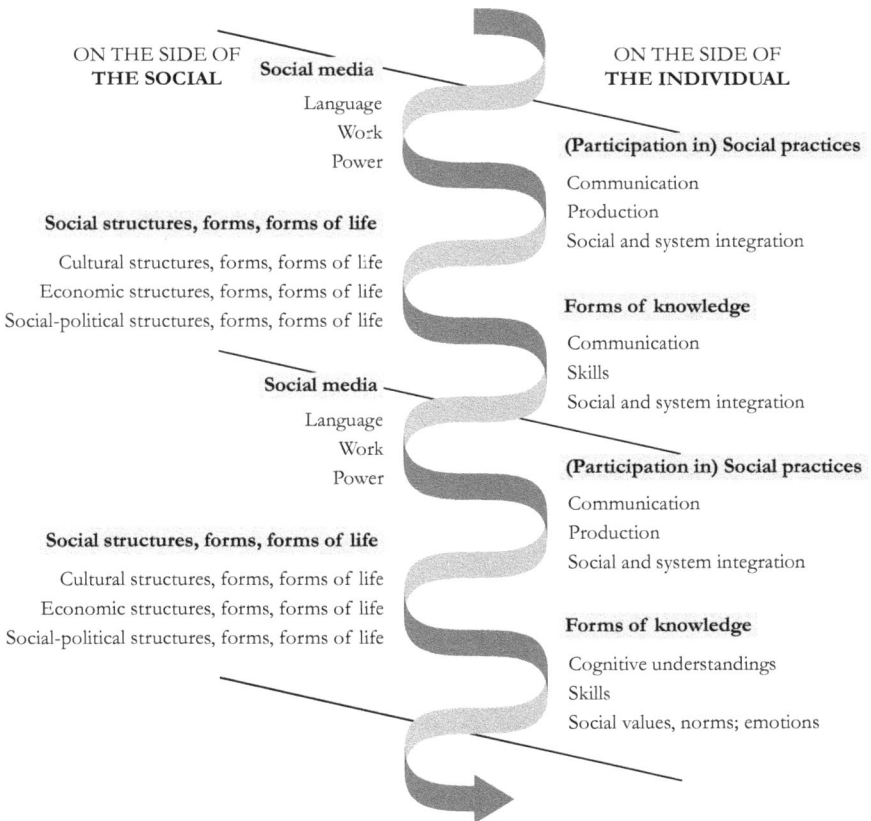

ON THE SIDE OF
THE SOCIAL   **Social media**
                                   Language
                                   Work
                                   Power

Social structures, forms, forms of life
Cultural structures, forms, forms of life
Economic structures, forms, forms of life
Social-political structures, forms, forms of life

                            Social media
                                   Language
                                   Work
                                   Power

Social structures, forms, forms of life
Cultural structures, forms, forms of life
Economic structures, forms, forms of life
Social-political structures, forms, forms of life

ON THE SIDE OF
THE INDIVIDUAL

(Participation in) Social practices
Communication
Production
Social and system integration

Forms of knowledge
Communication
Skills
Social and system integration

(Participation in) Social practices
Communication
Production
Social and system integration

Forms of knowledge
Cognitive understandings
Skills
Social values, norms; emotions

FIGURE 1.2. Relational Transformative Process of Participatory Action Research.

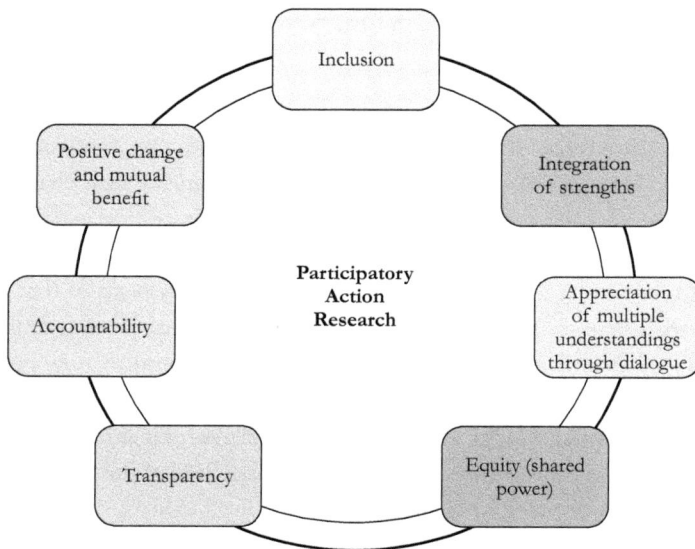

FIGURE 1.3. Participatory Action Research.

There are also a number of core values associated with action research, or participatory action research more specifically. Specifically, the research is an inclusive process that involves researchers as well as subjects. It also integrates the strengths of both in the process and as such would not be considered doing research to just answer a question, but rather it ties into strong social justice tenants that will lead to a positive change outcome. The seven core values are identified in Figure 1.3. These will be discussed in detail in Chapter 4.

By making a full circle, it is evident that action research is well suited for the social sciences and conforms to student interests in the social sciences. Since the value of students in the social sciences is to help people and/or be part of a change process, the adult learning principles support that value. The linking of action research to social science research then provides a more meaningful research experience that not only teaches research but helps students begin to see that research can be helpful to those in greatest need and can be part of a change process. The process involves populations in need, thus building on the basic concepts of looking at the person within the environment in order to assess, plan, act, and reflect. This provides a more meaningful and purposeful experience that the research brings to the learning experience. Although inferred in the diagram is the community where the action will take place, it is not explicit. This will be discussed in more detail in the later chapters of this book.

The next chapter will provide a history of action research, including our work and the development of participatory action research (PAR) and community-based participatory research (CBPR) to a newly created form that we are calling community-based participatory action research (CBPAR). The book will focus on techniques and strategies on how to conduct CBPAR based on our experiences. Chapter 3 will focus on how to define a community and understand the development of partnerships within the community and assess the power relationships. Chapter 4 will provide in-depth explanations of both PAR and CBPR, leading to Chapter 5 that will provide a step-by-step approach to CBPAR. Chapter 6 then describes CBPAR as a transformative process that utilizes the scientific method as a tool to build on interdisciplinary partnerships that lead to comprehensive change. Chapter 7 will discuss the ethical issues associated with this type of research, and some final thoughts will be shared in Chapter 8.

Rather than being just a theoretical approach to community-based participatory research, this text provides techniques and skills on how to conduct each of the aspects of CBPAR. In addition, these skills will be described in a context that was used to transform a community that led to some action being taken. As such, this text provides the "how" to transform change in addition to the "why."

Image Credits

Fig. 1.1: Stephen Kremmis and Robin McTaggart; The Action Research Spiral, from "Participatory Action Research: Communicative Action and the Public Sphere," *Handbook of Qualitative Research*, 2nd ed., ed. Norman K. Denzin and Yvonna S. Lincoln, pp. 278. Copyright © 2007 by SAGE Publications.

Fig. 1.2: Adapted from Stephen Kremmis and Robin McTaggart; Relational Transformative Process of Participatry Action Research, from "Participatory Action Research: Communicative Action and the Public Sphere," *Handbook of Qualitative Research*, 2nd ed., ed. Norman K. Denzin and Yvonna S. Lincoln, pp. 281. Copyright © 2007 by SAGE Publications.

Fig. 1.2a: Copyright © 2014 Depositphotos/cteconsulting.

Fig. 1.3: Darlyne Bailey, et al., "Participatory Action Research," The Alignment of Leadership Development and Participatory Action Research (PAR): One Process and Product From the University Northside Partnership. Copyright © 2009 by University of Minnesota.

CHAPTER 2

Historical Development of Community-Based Participatory Research

To FULLY UNDERSTAND community-based participatory research, it is important to begin with a very brief history of its development. Throughout time, researchers have been trying to gain an understanding or a meaning to why things are the way they are. The meanings of life, as I will call them, begin with an observation of events with a particular outcome that raises a question as to how that happened and if it can be replicated in order for it to happen again. These observations may be classified as either natural occurrences, such as that when I drop something it falls, thus demonstrating how gravity works, to social events, such as that when people feel as though someone is taking advantage of them, they rebel. These two different types of observations are classified either as natural sciences or social sciences.

The irony is that both types of inquiry for either the natural sciences or the social sciences follow a similar process; however, it is easier to control different variables when testing the natural sciences than it is to control variables with the social sciences. Therefore, a theory like gravity can be shown to be true almost 99% of the time whereas a social scientist is happy when the results are significant for around 20% of the time.

This discrepancy in proving something in the social sciences led to some of the early social scientists to see if there was a way to develop a grand theory that would try to explain everything. Talcott Parsons in the 1930s was one such person who built some of his observations on Weber's social action theory (Zaret, 1980). Briefly stated, Weber felt that empirical facts are selectively constructed by the theoretical interests of the persons who are constructing the facts (Zaret, 1980). Thus, in the social sciences, one cannot separate the researcher's values from the reporting of the observations (Simmel, 1982; Weber, 1949, 1975). This leads to Weber's views on social action because they involve the contextual factors that either hinder or promote the realization of values that relate to the expressed concepts (Zaret, 1980).

Parsons built on Weber's understanding that the actions involve the contextual factors based on cultural factors of the individual but differed by stating that the analysis of the event is not a logical account of the event (Zaret, 1980). As such, Parsons attempted to develop an analytic theory of action that converged science and action as a way of trying to minimize interpretation by being more rational.

While Weber and Parsons were trying to develop a grand theory to explain action, Kurt Lewin visited the Tavistock Institute of Human Relations in Great Britain in 1933 and 1936 where he learned the insight about approaches to action as part of community development (Kemmis & McTaggart, 2005). Upon his return to the United States, Lewin applied these concepts to community action programs. It was this work that led to the action research movement and the reason why Lewin is credited with being the father of action research.

It was not until there was recognition in Australia of the practical qualities of the action that leed a number of third-world countries to adapt the concepts into a "critical" and "emancipatory" nature that became noted as emancipatory action research. As a connection began to grow between emancipatory action research and participatory action research, a number of social movements in the developing world adopted these concepts to assist with their endeavors to establish a more equitable society. Most notably were Paulo Freire (Brazil), Orlando Fals Borda (Columbia), Rajesh Tandon (India), Anisur Rahman (Bangladesh), and Marja-Liisa Swantz (Tanzania) in applying the merged critical emancipatory action research and participatory action research into their social transformations.

Thus, two approaches to action research emerged. First, the development of theoretical arguments for more "actionist" approaches and, second, the need for participatory action research to link to broad social movements (Kemmis & McTaggart, 2005).

The emphasis of participatory action research then became associated with a social transformation process primarily focusing on change with third-world countries. It has its roots in neo-Marxist approaches to community development with liberal origins in human rights activism (Kemmis & McTaggart, 2005).

However, the radical nature of participatory action research was a little too radical for more centrist classroom and research approaches. Rather than focusing on major social transformations, it was felt that aspects can be applied on smaller scales, returning back to the Lewin influence of human relations and organizational change as identified through his work with the Tavistock Institute. Thus, for a number of years, there was an approach to look at the applications of action research in the classroom or in industry to address the need to improve organizational effectiveness and employee relations.

As environmental concerns began to rise, there was a need to engage the community and define, analyze, and prescribe solutions for the environmental health hazards that are affecting the residents of those communities, particularly the poor and persons of color (Corburn, 2002). Corburn identified this as community-based participatory research or CBPR, a process that engages community members as equal partners with scientists to arrive at a definition of the problem, a procedure for how to collect and analyze data, and then how to collectively develop an action plan for social change (Corburn, 2002).

Whereas participatory action research was a process of collaborative learning realized by groups of people who joined together to change the practices on how to interact, community-based participatory research began by engaging the community as equals in the process and developed shared processes on how to use the information to develop a plan. Both participatory action and community-based action research look at actual practices and not abstract practices. Both emphasize learning in real time, with the emphasis on particular people, places, and things. Both PAR and CBPR focus on addressing issues in the here and now and are aligned with qualitative research techniques in using the data to help create a planned social change that is of value to the people involved.

CHAPTER 3

Defining the Community

Partnerships and Power Relationships

T HE PREVIOUS CHAPTER introduced community-based participatory research (CBPR) as one model in the overarching umbrella of action research. That being said, an important aspect of CBPR is the engagement with the community.

However, community or defining community has become a little problematic recently. Technology has changed the way that we define or look at community, something that has been morphing since the 17th century when communities were self-sustaining and provided all functions for its members, something that Ferdinand Tönnies (1855–1936) called *gemeinschaft*. As societies moved into industrialization and people began leaving the comforts of their communities for opportunities in urban areas, not only were there geographic communities that might provide safety and security issues, but there became trade communities around professions. There also became spiritual communities to address people's belief system to answer questions about the unknown. Tönnies called this *gesellschaft*. In other words, as part of *gemeinschaft* every function needed for survival was contained within the existing community. However, as industrialization came about and people began seeing other opportunities, not everything was contained in the community, and people began branching out to have their needs met. This meant that there became multiple communities that people engaged in to meet their various needs. Tönnies called this *gesellschaft*, but as our lives become more complex the need for various communities expands with that complexity. For example, I may have a faith community, a housing community, a professional community, a work community, an exercise community, and various volunteer communities for each of the volunteer activities that I engage in. I am probably leaving some categories out, but you can see that the more complex your life becomes, the more potential communities that you will be involved in.

This becomes important when it comes time to begin thinking about community and which of the various communities you are demonstrating alliances to and at what time. Various technologies have made it easier for all of us to connect with others often in a virtual community. We now have Facebook, Instagram, LinkedIn, Twitter, What'sApp, and many more that are connected through social media.

Exercise

In thinking about community, it is now important to think about context. Take a moment and think about all of the communities with which you are associated. How are you defining them? Do they relate to any of the following?

- Culture and language
- Public institutions/agencies
- Shared stories/history/tradition
- Community groups
- Religious groups
- School or work
- Formal networks like clubs, organizations, unions
- Informal networks

Each one of these is a community. On a separate piece of paper, list all the communities that you have in your life and your association to that community.

Next, identify an issue that you are addressing within that community. These may range from a variety of problems or concerns, but they are issues that have been discussed and shared in the community.

Finally, identify what criteria your community is using to define and/or describe this problem or concern.

Do you see how complicated it can be to properly identify a community? These become some of the issues that are being faced when developing a community-based participatory research project. How is the community being defined and what are the specific issues that are to be addressed? CBPR involves engaging the community and identifying some type of action that is to be addressed with community engagement. As such, it is important to properly identify both the community and the appropriate action to be taken.

Community Mapping

There are a number of steps that are part of the community mapping process. Community mapping helps you define or describe what shapes the community. There are aspects like the culture, language, stories, or traditions of the community. What public institutions or agencies serve the community? Are there any particular community groups or informal networks that define it?

To obtain more information about the community, it is important to understand the various demographics factors that relate to the community. Thus, demographic information about age, income, racial/ethnic composition, and family status is very important to fully appreciate the composition. Also, it is important to understand the socioeconomic factors associated with the particular community. For example, are there particular health or health care issues? Does the community have access to health care? What type of housing exists in the community? Does the community have access to public transportation? Are there parks, school, religious institutions in the community? Are there supermarkets in the community? What types of crime exists? Many of these questions can be answered by looking at census data, public health data, and police crime reports. It is important to have a good understanding of as much background about the community as possible, as it will help provide some basic understanding about the issues you might encounter once you engage the community leaders. This process will help you to start identifying the opportunities and threats/challenges the community faces as well as make it more clear as to who is and is not represented in the community. This becomes important when we move to the power-mapping process of who is represented and who is not when it comes to the decision-making process to achieve some sort of change.

Once you have collected the data, you may want to begin a narrowing process to determine what you have the capability of doing. Community mapping can be very involved and time consuming. Therefore, it is helpful to narrow the scope to a specific task such as addressing the needs in a specific geographic area or focusing on a social issue. Since you are engaging community members, it is important to be flexible and open-minded as the process will evolve as you learn more about the community and the stakeholders involved. Throughout this process, it is important to keep two questions in mind: (a) Why am I collecting this information? and (b) What do I want to use it for?

The mapping process will identify a number of core constituencies, as well as other stakeholders and other potential allies. This process will identify who is affected by the issue and what you have to do to start engaging others. It is important to be able to assess who would be good potential coalition partners. The goal is to strategically build a coalition for the sake of achieving change. Most likely you will want to start with a small group of influential people. Think of the constituencies in concentric circles, starting with those individuals who are immediately with you. Then brainstorm to identify who is missing and should be at the table; these would be classified as **other stakeholders**. They are people who are deeply affected by the issue and would have the most interest in seeing a change. There are also those individuals who have a strong ideological interest in what you are doing, and they would be classified as **other potential allies**. The constituencies are depicted by Figure 3.1.

Now that we have identified the various constituencies, it is important to identify what assets are needed. A community asset is broadly defined as anything that can be used to improve the quality of community life. It can be a person who gets things done or a place where people can gather and meet to discuss what needs to be done. It could also be business that supports the community and is willing to participate in the change process. It can be a source of funding that supports the change process. It can also be a knowledgeable person who understands the change process or has access to the media, data, history of the community, or how the political process works. It is important to have people who have relationships and access to people in power in order for the change process to happen. More about power will follow.

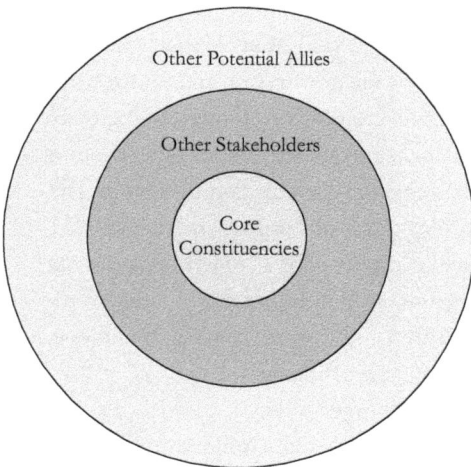

FIGURE 3.1. Finding Potential Allies.

Challenge

As a way to demonstrate community mapping, let's look at the issue of home-lessness. Homelessness is becoming a concern for many communities. However, the question is "What should be done to address the homeless problem in your community?" On the one hand, there is the business community that does not appreciate homeless people sleeping and urinating in the business entrances or harassing potential customers begging for handouts. On the other hand, there are individuals who have been devastated by circumstance and can no longer afford a roof over their heads and have been subjected to living on the streets. Many times, people have become homeless because of adverse childhood experiences (ACEs), mental illness, low self-esteem, discrimination, or substance abuse. There are many reasons, too many to identify and very personalized to the person, as to the reason for being homeless. However, the one commonality is that the homeless person has experienced a lot of defeat and has lost any sense of hope.

Your position is with the homeless collaborative or coalition, and city government has approached the coalition for solutions that would address the homeless problem. The business community wants them gone and out of sight, but that will not address the needs of the individuals who are homeless, and relocating them may only exasperate the problems that led to them being homeless in the first place. This becomes a little more complicated since many members of the homeless coalition are also affiliated with the business community and much of the funding comes from business. Also take into consideration that federal home-less dollars come to the collaborative, which then distributes those funds to the services of the same members of the collaborative that many homeless people tend to avoid since the homeless person feels that they are being judged for their situation by them. Thus, your task is to identify the community with which you are going to work and then develop the most appropriate action plan possible to address the community.

> Who is the community?
> What needs are you addressing by defining this community?
> Who is being left out by your decision?
> Who cares about your decisions?

Discuss with others about the decisions you made. How do they differ based on your definition of community and the needs of the population? Do you see how defining the community one way creates one perspective while defining the community a different way provides a different perspective with very different solutions?

Once you have defined your community, it is important to identify different tasks and outcomes. One way to achieve that is engaging the decision makers and conducting Lewin's force field analysis.

Lewin's Force Field Analysis

Lewin's force field analysis is a tool developed by Kurt Lewin in the 1940s that has become a dynamic tool for engaging stakeholders in the problem-solving process. A graphic of the tool is provided in Figure 3.2. The problem is identified in the middle. Above the problem is a list of all stakeholders affected by the change process. To the left of the problem everyone brainstorms the driving forces for change. To the right of the problem, everyone brainstorms the restraining forces that are preventing change. Once everything is listed, then the participants identify and prioritize strategies for change, engaging the stakeholders and acknowledging both driving and restraining forces.

As mentioned, Lewin's force field analysis is a good tool to engage participants from the community and involve them in the decision-making process. The tasks are helpful in developing the goals and objectives that are needed in developing a logic model for the next steps.

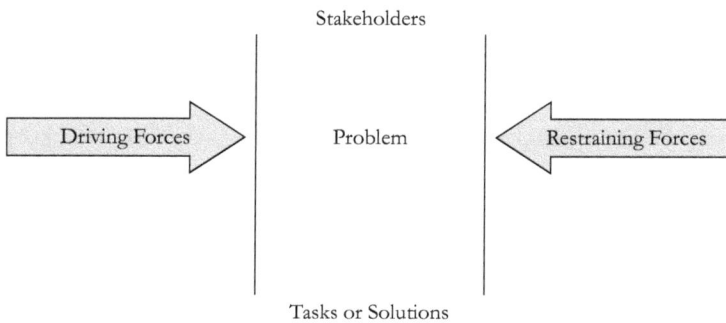

Stakeholders

Driving Forces ▷   Problem   ◁ Restraining Forces

Tasks or Solutions

FIGURE 3.2. Lewin's Force Field Analysis.

SWOT Analysis

Another useful tool is a SWOT analysis, which stands for strengths, weaknesses, opportunities, and threats (some people prefer C for challenges rather than threats as it sounds more strengths based). A SWOT analysis is a group technique, similar to Lewin's force field analysis. However, rather than addressing the change process from a purely change perspective, it addresses the capacity for change. This is accomplished by analyzing the internal **s**trengths and **w**eaknesses of the community coalition and then looking at the environmental factors within which the community operates—**o**pportunities and **t**hreats. Regarding the internal factors, it is important to identify the personnel in place, along with budget and structure. The environmental factors should consider prospective funders, stakeholders, competing services, and other factors that could be externally affecting a change process.

Logic Model

Once the data has been gathered, it would be helpful to create a logic model as a way of organizing the information to identify the short-term, mid-term, and long-term outcomes. Logic models are used to help identify the materials and processes needed to achieve the desired results. This can be a very useful way to organize, plan, and analyze, with the goal of achieving outcomes-based results. When the logic model is used in conjunction with Lewin's force field analysis, the brainstorming of what needs to be achieved and who is involved emerges from the force field and the SWOT analysis, the capacity for change, and then the strategies of how to achieve and what is needed to achieve becomes part of the logic model. Thus, the major recurring items and activities, along with short-term, mid-term, and final outcomes are identified on the logic model. A basic logic model diagram is depicted in Figure 3.3.

Inputs	Process/ resources	Outputs	Short-term outcomes	Intermediate outcomes	Long-term outcomes

FIGURE 3.3. Logic Model.

Power Analysis

Now that we have identified the community and the outcomes we hope to achieve through a change process, it is important to analyze who has the power to make that change and where the greatest resistance will be. A power analysis is an important tool in analyzing power relationships that will help develop a strategy for accomplishing the proposed outcomes. There are eight steps to a power analysis map. The map is depicted in Figure 3.4. The steps are as follows:

Step 1: Define the major problem(s) or condition(s) that are negatively affecting your constituencies. This step was accomplished as part of the community mapping process.

Step 2: Sketch the competing agendas (social justice versus corporate), the agenda of those who are causing or perpetuating the problem(s), and the community's agenda (conditions you want to bring about). This might be some of the restraining forces from Lewin's force field analysis.

Step 3: Sketch major issues/policy battles related to the problem/condition that are happening. This will be the overarching theme for the policy analysis map.

Step 4: Sketch the major decision-makers over the problem/condition. Stratify the participants on the left side of the power map (Figure 3.4). Those who are the most ardent would be the farthest to the left while those who are not as strident would be more centric. Those with the greatest influence would be to the top while those with the least power or influence would be toward the bottom.

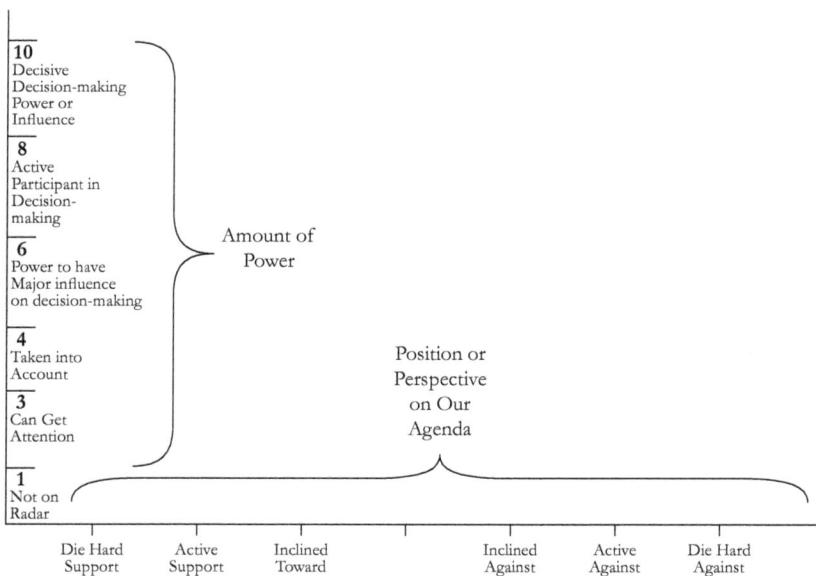

FIGURE 3.4. Power Analysis Map.

Step 5: Sketch major organized opposition. Stratify the participants on the right side of the power map (Figure 3.4). Those who are the greatest opposition would be the farthest to the right while those who are not as strident would be more centric. Those with the greatest influence would be to the top while those with the least power or influence would be toward the bottom.

Step 6: Sketch the organized progressive groups. Follow the same steps in step 4, only with groups.

Step 7: Sketch key unorganized social sectors. Follow the same steps in step 5, only with groups.

Step 8: Analyze the map and develop strategies for changing the equation. Some strategies will be identified next, such as information on elevator speeches.

The power analysis map or power map identifies the decision makers who need to be reached in order to achieve the predetermined outcomes that were identified in your logic model. Those individuals with the most influence will be at the top of the map while those with less influence will be closer to the bottom. Also, those individuals who are the greatest supporters will be to the far left, and those who are the most against will be to the far right. Those in the middle could be swayed either way. Similarly, the groups with the most influence will be at the top. One usually does not think of groups having much power; however, it is amazing to see the influence that such groups as Kiwanis or Rotary have on the decision makers in a community. The question, then, is how does a person become invited to be able to make a presentation about the problem to one of these groups with influential members in order for them to be engaged in the project.

Now that you have identified the power structure, it is important to develop a strategy on how to reach the decision makers. This section will introduce the ideas of how to make an elevator speech, how to write an op-ed, and how to provide testimony with the city council, county board, or school board.

Various Advocacy Tools

The power analysis map identified two different types of individuals—those who demonstrate some level of support for the cause and those who are opposed to the cause. Thus, it is important to identify the person with whom you are trying to connect and the type of message that you need to state in order to gain support. That means in some instances you will need to develop two different types of strategies, one for those individuals who already support the cause but you would like to obtain a more active level of support. A different strategy is needed for obtaining support for persons who begin by being opposed to the cause that you are promoting.

It is also important to realize that whatever messaging you are conveying, it needs to be succinct and to the point. There will be time for a longer discussion if you piqued the interest of the person that you are trying to engage. A number of years ago there was a commercial that used the tag line "You only have one chance to make a first impression." That tag line has stuck with me in relationship with engaging people for an advocacy project since it is important to realize that the first impression is important to develop a more lasting relationship.

Elevator Speech

An elevator speech is a brief statement about the cause that you are communicating. Envision that you entered an elevator with an important individual with whom you want to engage for your project. You only have the time together that it takes to ride the elevator from the bottom to the top or vice versa, from top to bottom, about 30 seconds. Hopefully you have prepared for such a meeting, but the bigger question is what you actually did to prepare. Take into consideration that you have 30 seconds or less, which equates to about 80 to 90 words or 8 to 10 sentences. What are the elements of those 8 to 10 sentences?

First, it is important to smile and open with a statement that grabs attention. Introduce yourself along with the organization that you represent and your role, making sure that you demonstrate enthusiasm about the topic. Identify a contribution that the organization has made to address the problem; an example is helpful. Make sure to explain how the other person can help identifying what they have to offer to the project. Ask for a longer meeting to be able to provide more in-depth details about the project and what the individual can do. The goal is to make an introduction and then be able to have a follow-up meeting to discuss the details. It is important to be passionate as to what the individual can do to contribute to the project. Make sure you have done your homework and know which side of the issue the individual represents for you to make the proper pitch that engages the individual for a longer meeting.

Although 30 seconds does not sound like a long time, if you have not prepared for your elevator speeches, 30 seconds can be an eternity, and you will not be successful in achieving your desired results. Therefore, it is important to be prepared. Write your thoughts down first, probably two sets, one for a supporter and a second for an opposer. Knowing the background of the individual will help you determine which speech to present.

Make sure that your message is simple and free of any jargon. These should be short but powerful statements meant to engage the individual to want to take action. Once you have your speeches written, then you need to practice. As stated, 30 seconds does not sound like a long time, so I think it is best to practice while standing on one foot. It becomes easy to drift and say unnecessary things, but balancing on one foot forces you to think about how you can state the important elements while holding your balance (this is only a practice technique like repeating your speech while looking at yourself in the mirror). To be invited to another longer meeting, make sure you have answered the question of "What is in it for them?" An exchange of business cards with how to follow up is important.

Providing Public Testimony

A very powerful tool is to provide public testimony at a public hearing. This may be at a school board, a city council meeting, or any legislative meeting where it is important to bring attention of a situation to people who have the power to create a policy that could address it. However, one should not just show up and begin speaking. It is important to be prepared and understand the roles of the body in which you plan to provide the testimony.

To begin the preparation process, it is important to ascertain how much time you will be granted to make your statement. Many open legislative meetings have a 2-minute time allotment where a light system is used to let you know how much time you have. A green light means you can speak, a yellow light is a warning that you only have about 15 seconds left and should begin wrapping up, while a red light means to end. It is not a good idea to push your luck and go beyond the red light because that might discount everything that was previously said.

It is important to then write down the ideas that you want to convey in that period of time. In writing your testimony, make sure that it is well organized and to the point, with effective transitions and a memorable closing statement. Be careful not to use jargon but keep the language and word choice simple. A basic outline might appear like the following:

    a.   Identify yourself and the organization you represent. It is perfectly okay to say you are a concerned citizen.

b. Acknowledge the group to whom you are providing the testimony.
c. Clearly state your position, for example you are supporting or opposed to a particular bill or practice.
d. Support your position with a factual argument and data as evidence.
e. The use of a personal experience makes the testimony very powerful because it provides a human-interest aspect. This is possibly the most memorable type of statement that will have a lingering effect on the decision-making group to whom you are providing the testimony.
f. Conclude by restating your position and encouraging them to take an action that was supported by your testimony.
g. Thank the group to whom you just provided the testimony for allowing you the opportunity to speak.

Once you have written your testimony, practice it out loud. Sometimes it is helpful to practice in front of a mirror or before other persons who may also be providing testimony. They can help you to make sure you do not go over the 2 minutes. As you practice, tweak the words for it to be easier to say and simpler for others to hear. Also think about the flow and rhythm. Try to repeat it without reading it. You may want to transfer your testimony to note cards or a single sheet of paper just to cue you on the points you want to make. Even though you may be very familiar with the content, stating it in front of a group of people is quite different than in front of a mirror. If you are planning to use a quote, it is okay to read the quote since that would be a direct, referenced statement. Timing is key. Rather than trying to speed up to say a lot, it is better to reduce what you want to say and slow down, using silence between ideas for greater affect.

On the day that you provide testimony, it is important to arrive early and sign up. The sessions have time for public testimony, and the order for providing the testimony usually follows the order that people signed up. Since there may be people who provided testimony before you, try not to repeat what has already been said but provide new information. This is where the use of a personal experience is useful since that experience is your experience. If someone from the decision-making body asks a question, answer as succinctly and accurately as you can. If you do not know the answer, state that you will get back to them after the meeting with the answer.

Do not argue with opposing views but keep to your facts and your points.

Op-Ed

An op-ed is a focused opinion that appears on or near a paper's editorial page, hence the name op-ed or opinion editorial. These are clearly stated (750 words) pieces that state a defined point of view. As such, it is important that the piece is written with a clear train of thought and with a strong, unique voice.

The op-ed is not just an opinion but is based on sound research about the topic, including facts, quotes, source data, and personal observation. For impact purposes, it is advisable to include sensory (touch, taste, smell, sound, or sight) data. As such, you might include field research from the site or interviews, along with academic research using secondary materials.

Since the op-ed is limited to 750 words, the beginning is critical. It is important to make a bold statement to grab the reader's attention. This can be accomplished by a strong claim, stating a surprising fact, using a metaphor, or a personal interest scenario. The beginning lays the foundation.

The middle includes the factual information, the data to support your position. It should not be too long but rather support the intent of the argument. This then builds to a strong ending.

The ending needs to echo the introduction in order to maintain the theme. You want to keep your most memorable detail in the ending. The ending should also lead to some type of call to action.

It is important to keep the tone free of jargon; the simpler or more understandable the piece, the better it will be received.

Whereas you are aware of your audience when stating an elevator speech or providing testimony, the audience for an op-ed piece is not known. There may be some basic assumptions of the audience based on the history of the newspaper, but in general this is a type of presentation that may have the widest reach. As such, once the op-ed is published, it is possible to electronically send a link to it to your email distribution groups. This will help bring attention to the piece and expand the distribution beyond the normal distribution of the paper.

The next chapter reviews the steps of community-based participatory research.

CHAPTER 4

CBPAR as a Research Process

T O THIS POINT we have provided an overview of action research and various alliances with action research as a process of focusing on a change process, the history of action research and various developments of action research, and a description of community and identifying power within the community with tools on how to approach the community to lead to a change process. Two models that are relevant to that change process are participatory action research (PAR) and community-based participatory research (CBPR). Many funders are requesting that you include a research model that follows one or the other of these two action research processes.

However, there appears to be some question about the differences between PAR and CBPR. Both are action research processes that involve taking some sort of action. However, there are some minor distinctions between the two. First, PAR is a five-step process that follows the steps of (1) problem identification, (2) data collection, (3) data analysis, (4) reporting data, and (5) taking action (Bailey et al., 2009). There is a perception that there is a community involved in the process to whom the report is made and where the action will happen. Although there is no explicit mention of community, the work with the community is inferred.

Participatory action research involves the first step to identify the problem, collect the data, analyze it, and then report to the action team before taking action. There are some basic assumptions that there is a community with whom the research involves but it is not formally part of the actual steps. This is one of the areas where community-based participatory research differs in that the community is formally engaged through the outlined steps.

Community-based participatory research (CBPR), on the other hand, is more explicit about the role of the community but less explicit about taking action. The eight (8) steps of CBPR are (1) define community, (2) engage community (needs assessment), (3) identify research questions, (4) design research/hypothesis, (5) identify roles and responsibilities in the research process, (6) conduct research, (7) analyze and interpret data, and (8) report results with taking action as being inferred. The first three steps in CBPR involve community engagement and working with the community to develop a community needs assessment. Thus, the front end of CBPR involves a number of community-engaged steps that make it more of a community-based process.

Once the community needs assessment is completed by working with the community members, the specific research questions are developed. Based on those questions, it is possible to prioritize them and begin to design a research process, including developing some assumptions or hypotheses and how to address them. This is the design phase.

During the design phase, along with the other phases, it is important to continue to be engaged with the community leaders. This helps with the building of trust and authenticity between you as the researcher and the community. Many community leaders steer away from researchers because there is the fear that the research is done to the community with very little engagement. Then a report is written, and the community never sees the benefit of allowing the researcher to collect data from the community. Thus, CBPR is very different in that the community continues to be engaged with the research team at all parts of the process.

Therefore, the research team will develop a strategy to address the questions that the community leaders have prioritized. Then the research team shares the process with the community leaders for discussion and approval of the plan. This is where roles and responsibilities of the research process will be shared, with the intent that community leaders will be involved with the data-collection process. Again, it is important to keep the community engaged with all aspects of the research process.

Once the data is collected, community leaders are involved with analyzing and interpreting the data. This will then lead to the final phase of the development of an action plan when the results are shared.

As is evident, PAR is more explicit on taking an action, while CBPR is focused more on the involvement of the community throughout the process. Both PAR and CBPR focus on action and community; it is just that they are described differently in their names. This leaves some room for the researcher to embrace a model that is unique and specific to their personality.

Another approach might be to create a blended model, called community-based participatory action research or CBPAR. This will integrate the aspects of both the action as well as how to engage the community and formally involve the community in the process. The next chapter builds on this new integrative model.

CHAPTER 5

Step-by-Step Approach to CBPAR

A S PREVIOUSLY MENTIONED, the differences between PAR and
CBPR might be minimal, but the focus of each is different, and it
is that difference that makes it important to integrate the two. First of all,
many times when I work in the community, I hear that the members of the
community are a little frustrated about feeling like the guinea pig and constantly providing information for a research university but never receiving
any feedback or seeing any real change happen. As such, it makes it difficult when an action researcher wants to engage the community in order
to address some problem and then engage the community in a change
process. Thus, making the first step is to build a trusting relationship with
the leaders of the community in order to proceed through a process that
leads to an action and eventually a change.

The value of community is so important, which is the reason for the sub-
title. However, as identified in Chapter 3, we live in a society where we are
simultaneously involved with multiple communities, some of which engage
and interact and others where the only interactions are you as the common
denominator between them. This means that the first step to any research will
need to be to define the community.

Step 1: Define the Community

Chapter 3 was very explicative about defining the community and developing a community map. It also provided information about the power structures within the community and how to reach out and engage the community, which is step 2 in the process.

Step 2: Engage the Community

Engaging the community is easier said than done. The first question is who to engage. It is always best to find some champions or people who will be supportive of your interests and can introduce you to the community. This would be similar to a snowball technique in identifying subjects for a research study. The big difference is that the people identified will be part of the community team that will help with the needs and with developing the systematic community needs assessment that develops the research questions.

There are a number of ways to conduct a systematic community needs assessment. It is important to work with your community partners to decide the best way to proceed. In essence, some of the ways to assess the needs of the community involve gathering opinions from key informants; collecting a variety of statistics depending on the issues that are being explored; looking at existing data from health departments, schools, or law enforcement; reviewing existing research about the incidence and/or prevalence of the problem; looking at the social determinants of health and their relationship to the community, such as income levels, poverty, age, home ownership, and so on; or conducting a survey of the community (Netting et al., 2017). The leadership team may decide that a combination of a number of these methods might be best to obtain an overall picture of the community. If at all possible, it is also a good idea to learn as much of the history about the community as possible. For example, when we applied for a Promise Neighborhood grant, we began by referencing John Steinbeck's *Grapes of Wrath*, since the community included the Weedpatch Camp that was referenced. The community was very appreciative that I was able to tell their story in relationship to applying for funding.

I find that one of the ways to engage and build trust in the community is to be genuine and to show interest in the community, including learning as much as you can about it. Learning about the community will also help with identifying the various power players, both supporters and opposers. This will help with the development of your elevator speeches, as identified in Chapter 3.

Part of the community needs assessment is to identify the assets or strengths in the community. These could be social as well as political assets. Many communities have a level of resiliency that can be used as a strength, which helps understand how the community handles adversity. In working in the colonias (undeveloped housing communities mostly in Texas, Arizona, and New Mexico) there was a concern about gang activity. We had a meeting with the sheriff to develop a neighborhood watch program. He said it was not a problem because they could call the department. I saw the expression on everyone's face and asked the sheriff to see how many had phones. Of the 20 people in the room, only one family had a phone. The sheriff was able to provide phones with only one number that would be accessed, the sheriff's department. Thus, one sees that communities can be resilient when they pull together.

A good assessment tool for doing a community needs assessment is a SWOT (strengths, weaknesses, opportunities, and threats) analysis that was mentioned in Chapter 3. It is also a good engagement tool that involves the community leaders in the assessment process.

Step 3: Identify the Problem

Upon completing the community needs assessment, there should be sufficient data, both qualitative and quantitative, depending on the types of assessment tools the community leaders chose, to analyze the data and to decide on what problems to address. This is a reflective process and involves all parties. Through the process, community leaders can begin to prioritize what is realistic and what is not. This process leads to the development of what classic researchers call research questions, or things that you would like to see changed.

This process involves the values of the community blended with the critical thinking—problem-solving processes of a researcher. It also creates a very dynamic exchange. As previously mentioned, one of the frustrations of many community leaders is that academic institutions want to study them but there is very little engagement in what should be studied. Thus, this process is very dynamic by engaging and involving the community leaders in just what should be explored and how it should be explored. It also provides the community with a framework on what to do with the information.

Step 4: Design the Research and Identify Roles

Now that the problem has been identified, it is time for you as a researcher to work with the community to identify the best way to address the problem. This may involve some qualitative or quantitative analysis, or a combination of both techniques. A good way to begin may be to review the literature to see how others have addressed the problems. You might want to refer to Friedman (2017) for more specifics on how to transform a research question into a research study. In essence, the structure of the questions might dictate whether you are intending to do explanatory, descriptive, or exploratory research. Regardless, the goal is that the information will be used so that some action will be taken.

As also stated, this action involves the community. As such, it is important to share your ideas with the community and engage the community leaders in the data collection as much as possible. This is important since the more engaged the community is, the greater the ownership they will have to the findings, and those findings will have greater meaning for them. This also means that the action plan will be implemented with little or no involvement from you. Finally, this also reduces the complaints that many communities have about researchers in that they collect the data and leave with little investment in the community. Here, the community is engaged and involved with ownership to the process.

Step 5: Collect Data

With roles and responsibilities shared with others and a plan to collect the data, it is time to proceed. An important step, though, is to make sure everyone has been properly trained in the data-collection process. This might involve working with the local institutional review board (IRB) to see what steps need to be taken to make sure everyone is trained adequately to be able to satisfy the IRB. For example, prior to collecting data for the homeless point-in-time study, I went to the IRB and asked how to proceed. The local IRB felt comfortable by conducting a 4-hour training that everyone had to complete prior to collecting data. This covered the basic elements of the Belmont Report: respect for the person, beneficence, and justice (Friedman, 2017). The research design had been submitted to the IRB along with the survey instrument that was being used, both English and Spanish versions as well as sheltered and unsheltered versions. Thus, the data collection phase does involve some planning and behind-the-scenes work from you as the researcher in order to be prepared.

This is important information to share with the community leaders and helps them understand the elements of the process. Also, by involving them in an IRB training gives them more of a sense of ownership to the process.

Step 6: Analyze and Interpret Data

Depending on the types of data that were collected, the analysis phase takes some effort and understanding of what you found in relationship to the research questions. On the one hand, if the data was time related or past and current times were compared to see if there was any change or improvement, then the comparison might be easier to see. On the other hand, if you are looking at qualitative data, then the analysis might take a little longer. Hopefully, the interview or focus group questions were clear at the outset to identify some themes. If it was observational data, then there should have been some understanding prior to observing. These are all elements of qualitative data collection and not part of this text but something to be aware prior to beginning the data collection.

All along, the discussion has been about involving the community leaders in the aspects of the research process, and data is no different. Understanding and interpreting the data is usually done through the lens of the person doing the review. As such, the community leaders might have a slightly different take on the data than an outsider. If you recall, working with the community leaders in the colonias to create a neighborhood watch, the sheriff provided a hotline number that went directly to his office. The problem was the sheriff made an assumption that everyone had a telephone to make the call. His perception was different than the reality in the community. Thus, it is important to gain that additional insight by having the community leaders be part of the data-analysis process since their perceptions may be different than yours as a researcher.

Step 7: Report Results, Develop an Action Plan, and Take Action

I chose to combine reporting the data and developing an action plan in the same step since data without action is just data. I chose to combine the reporting and action plan as a single step since by reporting the data is the beginning process of the development of an action plan. The data is suggesting an action and that means that the contextual aspect of reporting the data will suggest the action that the analysis of the data suggests needs to happen.

Since all the steps along the way have involved the community leaders in a more intimate process, this step is no different. Since the community leaders have been engaged with all the steps including this one, reporting the results should provide nothing that has already been discussed and described. The tough part is the "So what?" question or "What do we do with all this information?"

In doing any type of research, it is always important to maintain focus on the question or problem that you are trying to resolve. This research is no different. What is different is the process to proceed.

As previously mentioned, the Kern High School District had a disproportionately high rate of suspensions and expulsions among students of color. The data identified that punitive measures were not addressing the problem, and the community leaders identified three alternative actions rather than the suspension and expulsion forms that were being used. The community would have preferred a restorative justice approach. Face-to-face meetings with the administrators were held, but there did not appear to be much movement from what was currently being done. As a result, the community leaders chose to bring suit against the district. Of course, the legal route creates a somewhat adversarial approach that most people try to avoid, but in this instance it was necessary. After 2 years in the court system, the courts found in favor of the community and mandated that the district take a different approach. Rather than restorative justice, the district chose a school-wide positive behavior support (SWPBS) approach.

I personally find that one of the best ways to identify the action plan to take is by completing Lewin's force field analysis, as described in Chapter 3. This process engages community leaders in developing the right actions steps with priorities, looking at the driving forces of why an action should be taken, along with the restraining forces as to why it will not happen.

Thus, the scenario just explained with the school district did not begin with a legal process but ended that way only after the nonlegal negotiations failed. A force field analysis helps with designing those steps and continues the engagement with community leaders.

Summary

This chapter provided a model for a seven-step process that combines elements of both PAR and CBPR. It keeps the community engaged at all times and involves them with the decision-making processes as well as the power to carry out the data-collection and analysis processes. By continually engaging the community, there is a reduction in feeling that the community is just a guinea pig for researchers.

CHAPTER 6

CBPAR a Transformative Process

Action research by design, and CBPAR is no exception, is a transformative process. By transformative, the intent is that something is going to change. What has been identified is that there are members of a community who feel that there is a problem. It is the leadership of that community who want to make a change so that the problem is resolved. By definition, that is a transformation.

However, how that transformation takes place might be a little different than normal processes. Through CBPAR, the community is key, and, as such, a mechanism is created that builds on a process that engages academics and community leaders to create a comprehensive change process. This is not purely science or a scientific process but rather is a collaborative involvement that relies on the expertise of all parties involved.

John Flanagan (1954) wrote a classic piece entitled *Critical Incident Technique* where the qualitative researcher would listen to the subjects, not to dictate what they should be doing but rather to listen and understand the subject as an expert of their own experience. As such, the researcher enters into an equal partnership with each subject to learn and identify commonalities that might exist in their experiences that can then be generalized to see if any trends emerge.

CBPAR is similar in that the researcher listens to the community leaders to understand how they perceive the problem, not to dictate what to do but to rather, as an objective person, to begin to parse it all together and design a research process to address and develop a planned change process that will transform the community by addressing the perceived needs.

This interdisciplinary relationship creates a comprehensive change process that engages all aspects of both the community and the academy. As more people become involved, the greater the knowledge base and the greater potential for building a truly transformative change process.

This is a dynamic process that breaks down the silos and also involves members of the academy with the community in a very interactive and supportive way to build knowledge. As such, the ownership is shared and the change is dynamic and transformative.

CHAPTER 7

Ethical Considerations

M AINTAINING THE ETHICAL foundation of any research process is key. Throughout my career, I have heard that there are a number of community members who state that the big research universities come into their communities, collect data, and then they never hear from them. They constantly use the term *guinea pig* in that they feel they are being used but never see any type of action or change as a result of being studied.

CBPAR is very different. It is all about the community. The community is engaged and is an equal partner in the research process. As such, there is no question about who owns the data or about what is happening with it. There is an action outcome that is expected, but that action involves the community in the process of change.

By maintaining the community as an equal partner, the three elements of the Belmont Report—respect, beneficence, and justice—will be maintained. Of course there is the need to minimize the risk to all subjects: making sure that the risk will be reasonable in relationship to the benefits; that the selection of the subjects is equitable; that all subjects are provided with documentation and sign that they are willingly participating in the study; that the data is monitored for safety of the subjects; that privacy is maintained for confidentiality;

and that there is no coercion or undue influence applied to the subjects (Friedman, 2017).

The key is that the community is an equal partner in the research process and engaged in all phases. As such, there should be no question about the rationale behind the research and who will benefit from this equal partnership.

CHAPTER 8

Last Words

LIKE ALL ACTION research, the focus is on the action. It is not like traditional research where the goal is to answer a question or prove a hypothesis, but the purpose is to identify an action that will transform a problem that exists in the community. In this instance, the community is an equal partner and is engaged in all aspects of the process.

Identifying the community is a difficult process, just like identifying a researchable question is difficult. However, the ultimate benefit for everyone is getting to develop an authentic relationship with a community and beginning to see the enthusiasm as the community begins to experience the transformation that things can be transformed.

The focus on social work is to provide hope to the clientele. Community-based participatory action research is all about providing hope to the community that a transformation will take place and that they are involved in that process.

REFERENCES

Bailey, D., Koney, K. M., Uhly, K., Bediako, T., Bruin, M., Hetler, J., Kivnick, H., McDowell, A., Milon, B., Propes, B., & Zulu-Gillespie, M. (2009). The alignment of leadership development and participatory action research (PAR): One process and product from the University Northside Partnership. University Northside Partnership and University of Minnesota, Urban Research and Outreach/Engagement Center in the Office for System Academic Administration.

Corburn, J. (2002). Combining community-based research and local knowledge to confront asthma and subsistence-fishing hazards in Greenpoint/Williamsburg, Brooklyn, New York. *Environmental Management, 29*, 451–466.

Flanagan, J. C. (1954). The critical incident technique. *Psychological Bulletin, 54*(4), 1–33.

Friedman, B. D. (2013). *How to teach effectively: A brief guide* (2nd ed.). Lyceum Books.

Friedman, B. D. (2017). *The research tool kit: Problem-solving processes for the social sciences*. Cognella.

Grundy, S. (1987). *Curriculum: Product or praxis*. Falmer Press.

Grundy, S. (1988). Three modes of action research. In S. Kemmis & R. McTaggert (Eds.), *The action research reader* (3rd ed.) (pp. XX–XX). Deakin University Press.

Grundy, S., & Kemmis, S. (1981). *Educational action research in Australia: The state of the art*. Paper presented at the Annual Meeting of the Australian Association for Research in Education, Adelaide, Australia.

Hacker, K. (2013). *Community-based participatory research*. SAGE.

How to Write an OP-ED or Column downloaded from Harvard Kennedy School January 25, 2017.

Kemmis, S., & McTaggart, R. (2007). Participatory action research: Communicative action and the public sphere. In N. K. Denzin & Y. S. Lincoln (Eds), *Handbook of qualitative research* (2nd ed.) (pp. XX–XX). SAGE.

Knowles, M. S. (1980). *The modern practice of adult education.* Cambridge Books.

Levin, M., & Greenwood, D. (2011). *Handbook of qualitative inquiry.* SAGE.

Lewin, K. (1946). Action research and minority problems. *Journal of Social Issues, 2*(4), 34–46.

McCutcheon, G., & Jung, B. (1990). *Alternative perspectives on action research. Theory Into Practice, 24*(3), 144–151.

Netting, F. E.; Kettner, P. M.; McMurtry, S. L.; & Thomas, M. L. (2017) *Social Work Macro Practice,* 6th ed. Pearson Education, Inc.

Rapaport, R. N. (1970). Three dilemmas in action research. *Human Relations, 23*(6), 499–513.

Sagor, R. (2000). *Guiding school improvement with action research.* Association for Supervision and Curriculum Development.

Simmel, G. (1917). *Fundamental problems of sociology.* Free Press.

Taggart, G. L., & Wilson, A. P. (2005) *Promoting reflective thinking in teachers: 50 action strategies* (2nd ed.). Corwin.

Weber, M. (1949). *Methodology of the social sciences.* Free Press.

Weber, M. (1975). *The logical problems of historical economics.* Free Press.

Zaret, D. (1980). From Weber to Parsons and Schutz: The eclipse of history in modern social theory. *American Journal of Sociology, 85*(5), 1180–1201.

INDEX

A

accountability, 6
action research, 6. *See also* community-based participatory action research (CBPAR); research
    collaborative, 3
    collective, 3
    critical analyses, 3
    described, 2
    methodological approach, 3
    reflective process, 5
    relational transformative process of, 5
    requirements, 4
    self-reflective, 3
    spiral, 4
adult learning, 2
adverse childhood experience (ACE), 17
advocacy tools of community, 21–22
analyze and interpret data, 28, 35–36
appreciation, 6

B

Borda, O. F., 10

C

challenges of community, 17–18
collaboration, 3
collaboratively learning, 11
community
    action programs, 10
    advocacy tools, 21–22
    aspects, 15
    challenge, 17–18
    described, 13–16
    development, 10
    elevator speech, 22–23
    logic model, 19
    mapping, 15–21
    members, 11
    op-ed, 25–26
    power analysis, 19–21, 20
    public testimony, 23–24
    skill set, 5
    SWOT analysis, 18
    target systems, 5
community-based participatory action research (CBPAR), 3, 7. *See also* community
    analyze and interpret data, 28, 35–36
    approaches, 31–36
    collect data, 34
    conduct research, 28
    define community, 28, 32
    design research/hypothesis, 28
    differences between PAR and, 31
    engage community, 28, 32–33
    ethical considerations, 41–42
    history of development of, 9–11
    identify research questions, 28, 33
    identify roles and responsibilities in research process, 28, 34–35
    relational transformative process of, 5
    report results, 28, 35–36

47

R

Rahman, A., 10
reporting data, 27
research. *See also* action research; community-based participatory action research (CBPAR); participatory action research (PAR)
    for action, 3
    in action, 4
    on action, 3
    adult learning styles, 2
    defined, 1
    methods/statistics course, 2
    problem-solving process, 1
    quantitative approach, 1
    social sciences, 1–2, 6, 9–10
Rotary group, 21

S

school-wide positive behavior support (SWPBS), 36
social change, 3
social constructs, 5
social problems, 2
social sciences
    described, 2
    elements of, 3
    level of methodological diversity, 2
    multi-perspective research approach, 2
    research. *See* research
    social problems, 2
    social scientists, 9
    stakeholders, 2
    student interests in, 6
    value of student in, 6

    variables, 9
social scientists, 9
stakeholders, 2, 16, 19
Steinbeck, J., 32
stories, 15
Swantz, Marja-Liisa, 10
SWOT analysis, community, 18

T

taking action, 27
Tandon, R., 10
Tavistock Institute of Human Relations in Great Britain, 10–11
Tönnies, F., 14
traditions, 15
transparency, 6

W

Weber, M., 10
Weber's social action theory (Zaret), 10

Lightning Source UK Ltd.
Milton Keynes UK
UKHW020617060821
388386UK00006B/256

9 781516 590629